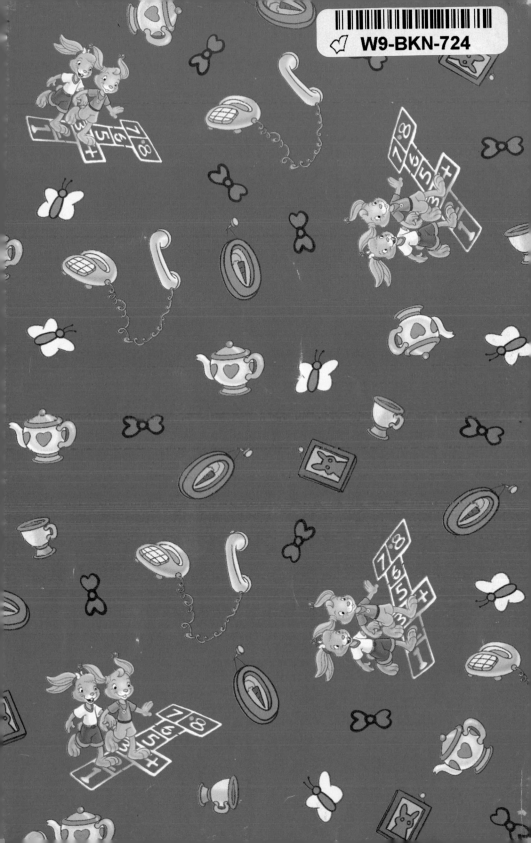

Dear Parents/Caregivers:

Children learn to read in stages, and all children develop reading skills at different ages. **Fisher-Price® Ready Reader Storybooks™** were created to encourage children's interest in reading and to increase their reading skills. The stories in this series were written to specific grade levels to serve the needs of children from preschool through third grade. Of course, every child is different, so we hope that you will allow your child to explore the stories at his or her own pace.

Book 1 and Book 2: Most Appropriate For Preschoolers

Book 3 and Book 4: Most Appropriate For Kindergartners

Book 5 and Book 6: Most Appropriate For First Graders

Book 7 and Book 8: Most Appropriate For Second Graders

Book 9 and Book 10: Most Appropriate For Third Graders

All of the stories in this series are fun, easy-to-follow tales that have engaging full-color artwork. Children can move from Books 1 and 2, which have the simplest vocabulary and concepts, to each progressive level to expand their reading skills. With the **Fisher-Price® Ready Reader Storybooks™**, reading will become an exciting adventure for your child. Soon your child will not only be ready to read, but will be eager to do so.

Educational Consultants: Mary McLean-Hely, M.A. in Education: Design and Evaluation of Educational Programs, Stanford University; Wendy Gelsanliter, M.S. in Early Childhood Education, Bank Street College of Education; Nancy A. Dearborn, B.S. in Education, University of Wisconsin-Whitewater

Fisher-Price® Ready Reader Storybook™

Best Friends  Book 9

Written by Susan Wallach • Illustrated by Paul E. Nunn

Modern Publishing
A Division of Unisystems, Inc.
New York, New York 10022

Becca and I have been best friends forever.

We have fun together.
Sometimes we pretend
we're sisters!

We love bubble gum and Halloween.

Last year we were mermaids.

9

When we grow up, we're
going to take care of the
elephants and ostriches at the zoo.

We don't like monsters!
But we love our clubhouse.

It's almost my birthday. Instead of a party we will have a sleepover.

We'll stay up all night. We'll wear
my mother's old gowns.

We both think my older
sister Alice is bossy.

She gets everything she wants.
She has her own phone and stereo.

Becca and I never hang out
with Alice. She's always too
busy doing grown-up things.

Becca and I
think Alice is silly.

But, lately, Becca wants to talk to Alice when she calls.

They meet after school.
They whisper and giggle.

My sister has everything.
And now she has my best friend!

I have no one to play with after school. Becca is too busy being Alice's best friend.

Worst of all, my birthday is tomorrow. How can I have a sleep-over without a friend to sleep over?

My family gives me gifts, but I don't care because Becca isn't my best friend anymore.

I don't care that my father takes me
to the zoo to see the baby ostrich.

I don't care that nobody's home when we return.

"Surprise!" Becca and Alice
have been planning my surprise
birthday party all week.

But the best gift is
that Becca and I are
still best friends!

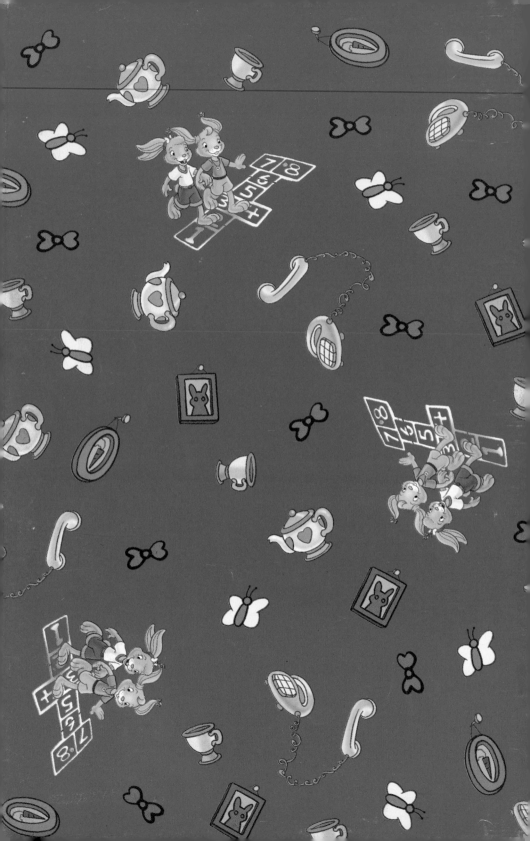